Charter Mark
Awarded for excellence
to Arts & Libraries

Kent
County
Council

WHY DO ANIMALS HAVE

SKIN, SCALES and SHELLS

Elizabeth Miles

HEINEMANN
LIBRARY

H **www.heinemann.co.uk/library**
Visit our website to find out more information about **Heinemann Library** books.

To order:
☎ Phone 44 (0) 1865 888066
▤ Send a fax to 44 (0) 1865 314091
▯ Visit the Heinemann Bookshop at www.heinemann.co.uk/library to browse our catalogue and order online.

First published in Great Britain by Heinemann Library, Halley Court, Jordan Hill, Oxford
OX2 8EJ, a division of Reed Educational and Professional Publishing Ltd. Heinemann is a registered trademark of Reed Educational & Professional Publishing Limited.

OXFORD MELBOURNE AUCKLAND JOHANNESBURG BLANTYRE
GABORONE IBADAN PORTSMOUTH NH (USA) CHICAGO

Designed by David Oakley@Arnos Design
Originated by Dot Gradations
Printed in Hong Kong

ISBN 0 431 15325 6
06 05 04 03 02
10 9 8 7 6 5 4 3 2 1

British Library Cataloguing in Publication Data

Miles, Elizabeth
    Why do animals have skin, scales and shells
    1.Skin - Juvenile literature 2.Scales (Fishes) - Juvenile literature
    3.Shells - Juvenile literature 4.Physiology - Juvenile literature
    I.Title
    573.5'1

Acknowledgements
The Publishers would like to thank the following for permission to reproduce photographs:
BBC NHU/Torsten Brehm p. 19; BBC NHU/Anup Shah p. 21; BBC NHU/David Welling p. 8; BBC NHU/Ingo Arndt p. 23; BBC NHU/Pete Oxford p. 28; BBC NHU/Peter Blackwell p. 13; Bruce Coleman Collection/Dr Eckart Pott p. 12; Bruce Coleman Collection/Hans Reinhard pp. 6, 26; Bruce Coleman Collection/John Cancalosi p. 29; Bruce Coleman Collection/Kim Taylor p. 24; Bruce Coleman Collection/Pacific Stock p. 14; Bruce Coleman Collection/Robert Maier p. 11; Bruce Coleman Collection/Staffan Widstrand p. 7; Corbis pp. 20, 27; Corbis/Charles Philip 22; Digital Stock p. 16; digital vision pp. 17, 30; NHPA/Anthony Bannister p. 9; NHPA/Morten Strange p. 10; OSF/Konrad Wothe p. 25; OSF/Mark Hamblin p. 5; OSF/Paul McCullagh p. 18; OSF/Root Okapia p. 15; Photodisc p. 4.

Cover photograph reproduced with permission of Oxford Scientific Films/John Mitchell.

Our thanks to Claire Robinson, Head of Visitor Information and Education at London Zoo, for her help in the preparation of this book.

Every effort has been made to contact copyright holders of any material reproduced in this book. Any omissions will be rectified in subsequent printings if notice is given to the Publisher.

Contents

Words in bold, **like this**, are explained
in the Glossary.

Why do animals have skin?

Skin is the outside layer of your body. It is thin and soft but protects your body. Many animals have skin to protect them. Some animals' skin is covered in hair or feathers.

Animals have all sorts of different body coverings. Some have soft coverings like our skin, others have harder coverings like scales and shells. This iguana has a scaly skin.

Smooth, wet skin

A frog has smooth, **moist** skin. Frogs are **amphibians**, which means they live both in and out of water. Their special skin protects them in water and on land.

Salamanders are amphibians, too. Young
salamanders breathe through **gills**. They can
also breathe through their skin.

Skins with poisons

Many **amphibians** have poison in their skin. This puts off **predators** who try and eat them. A cane toad has special **glands** behind its eyes. Poison flows from these glands through its skin.

Some small frogs have poison in their skin.
Bright colours and special markings on this
tree frog's skin warn predators of the
poison. They do not try and eat it.

Underwater skin

Some animals live underwater all the time. They have special skin to protect them and to keep the water out. An eel has a tough, slippery skin. Its skin helps to protect it from the bites of **predators**.

A humpback whale has thick skin. A layer of fat called blubber lies under the whale's skin. The thickness of the skin and the layer of blubber help to keep the whale's body warm in the cold sea.

Fish scales

A fish is protected by lots of tiny, overlapping pieces called scales. They are an extra covering over its skin. The scales also keep the water out of its body.

Fish scales are tough but make a very **flexible**, bendy covering. The fish can curve, twist and turn as it swims. It can move easily because the covering of scales is bendy.

Dry, scaly skin

Reptiles such as chameleons have scaly skin. The scales are not separate pieces, like fish scales. Instead, they form one complete layer. Scales protect a reptile's body from drying out in hot places like **deserts**.

Snakes are reptiles. Their belly scales stop them sliding backwards when they move. The scales also stop their bodies from getting scratched or worn as they move over tree branches, rocks and stones.

Shedding scaly skins

Lizards and snakes grow bigger all through their life, but their skins don't grow with them. They have to **shed** their scaly skins.

A snake sheds its skin many times during its life. The skin comes off in one piece. Underneath the old skin is a new, larger skin.

Plates and shells

Some **reptiles**, like crocodiles, have bony plates under their scales. This makes the scales stronger. These stronger scales are on the crocodile's back.

A tortoise's shell is made of bone with huge scales on top. Its head and legs are covered in smaller scales. The tortoise can pull its head and legs into its shell.

Other types of shells

A snail has a **coiled** shell. If there is danger nearby, the snail disappears completely into its shell. The shell also stops the snail's body from drying out.

Birds' eggs have hard, outer shells. Inside the shell, a chick grows until it is big enough to **hatch**. The shell protects the growing chick. It stops the chick and its food inside the egg from drying out.

Sea shells

All sorts of sea animals have shells to protect their soft bodies. A limpet's shell is like a wide cone. When the tide is out, a limpet holds fast to a rock.

A giant clam has a shell that is made up of two matching parts. They are joined at one side, so that the shell can open and close.

Underwater armour

Crabs have a hard outer covering, like armour. It is called an **exoskeleton**. It protects the crabs when they are washed by the sea on to rocky shores. It also protects them from **predators**.

As crabs and lobsters grow, their
exoskeleton gets too small for them.
They must crawl out of it and hide until
their new armour grows and hardens.

Armoured insects

Insects have small bodies that could easily dry out in the air. A ladybird is an insect. Like all insects, its tough **exoskeleton** stops its body from drying out when it flies.

A cockroach has a hard exoskeleton. This makes it difficult for other animals to attack. The exoskeleton covers its body, wings and legs.

Armoured mammals

Some **mammals** have amazing armour to keep them safe. A pangolin has overlapping horny scales over its body and tail. It curls up into a tough ball if another animal attacks it.

Armadillos have bony plates on their backs for protection. Some armadillos can roll themselves up into a ball. Now, every soft part of its body is protected.

Fact file

- The giant clam has the largest shell of all **molluscs**. It can measure more than one metre across.

Blue poison dart frogs have poisonous skin.

- Hermit crabs, do not have an **exoskeleton**. To protect their soft bodies, they hide in shells that once belonged to molluscs.

- Some fish, like puffer fish, have spiny scales to frighten away **predators**.

Glossary

amphibians   animals that can live on land and in water

coiled   rolled around in smaller and smaller circles

desert   very dry land, which may be very hot or very cold

exoskeleton   hard outer covering on a crab or insect's body

flexible   bendy and able to move easily

gills   parts of its body that a fish uses to breathe

glands   soft parts in a body that ooze a liquid

hatch   break out of an egg

insects   small animals with six legs and three parts to their body

mammals   animals that feed their babies with the mother's milk. People are mammals.

moist   a bit wet or damp

molluscs   animals protected by one or two shells, like snails and clams

predators   animals that hunt other animals for food

reptiles   animals such as snakes, lizards, crocodiles and tortoises

shed   allow to fall off

Index

Titles in the *Why Do Animals Have* series include:

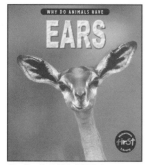

Hardback 0431 15311 6

Hardback 0431 15310 8

Hardback 0431 15326 4

Hardback 0431 15323 X

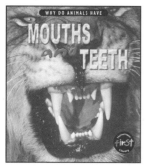

Hardback 0431 15314 0

Hardback 0431 15312 4

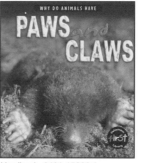

Hardback 0431 15322 1

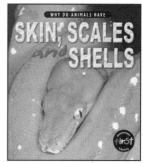

Hardback 0431 15325 6

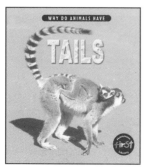

Hardback 0431 15313 2

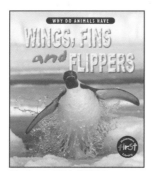

Hardback 0431 15324 8

Find out about the other titles in this series on our website www.heinemann.co.uk/library